DATE DUE

FAMOUS FIGURES OF

DAVY CROCKETT

THE AMERICAN FRONTIER

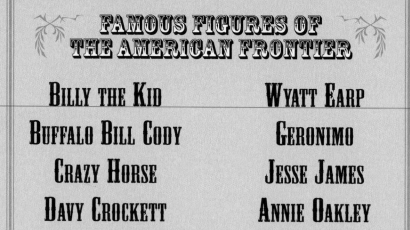

FAMOUS FIGURES OF
THE AMERICAN FRONTIER

BILLY THE KID	WYATT EARP
BUFFALO BILL CODY	GERONIMO
CRAZY HORSE	JESSE JAMES
DAVY CROCKETT	ANNIE OAKLEY
GEORGE CUSTER	SITTING BULL

FAMOUS FIGURES OF

DAVY CROCKETT

THE AMERICAN FRONTIER

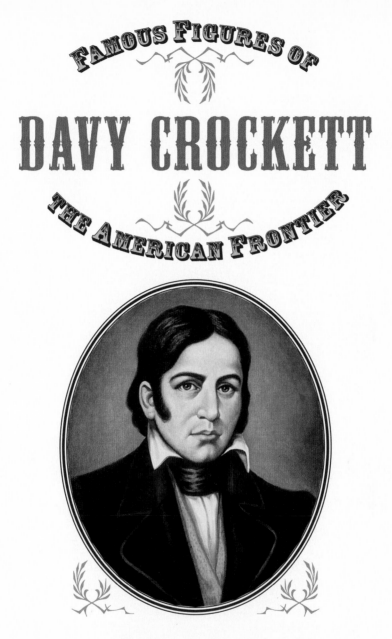

DANIEL E. HARMON

CHELSEA HOUSE PUBLISHERS
PHILADELPHIA

Produced for Chelsea House by
OTTN Publishing, Stockton, NJ

CHELSEA HOUSE PUBLISHERS
Editor in Chief: Sally Cheney
Associate Editor in Chief: Kim Shinners
Production Manager: Pamela Loos
Art Director: Sara Davis
Series Designer: Keith Trego

First Printing

1 3 5 7 9 8 6 4 2

The Chelsea House World Wide Web address is
http://www.chelseahouse.com

Library of Congress Cataloging-in-Publication Data

Harmon, Daniel E.
Davy Crockett / by Daniel E. Harmon.
    p.   cm. – (Famous figures of the American frontier)
Includes bibliographical references and index.
    ISBN 0-7910-6481-6 (hc: alk. paper)
    ISBN 0-7910-6482-4 (pbk.: alk. paper)
1. Crockett, Davy, 1786-1836–Juvenile literature. 2. Pioneers–
Tennessee–Biography–Juvenile literature. 3. Frontier and pio-
neer life–Tennessee–Juvenile literature. 4.
Tennessee–Biography–Juvenile literature. 5. Legislators–
United States–Biography–Juvenile literature. 6. United States
Congress. House–Biography–Juvenile literature. [1. Crockett,
Davy, 1786-1836. 2. Pioneers. 3. Legislators.] I. Title. II.
Series.

F436.C95 H37 2001
976.8'04'092–dc21   2001028846

CONTENTS

A painting of Davy Crockett waving farewell, carrying his long rifle and accompanied by his hunting hounds. Although most people think of Crockett as a great woodsman, he was also an important political leader during the 1820s and 1830s.

Boy of the Woods

Don't believe everything you hear about Davy Crockett. Yes, he was indeed a bold, wise, and skillful *buckskin*-clad American pioneer. He also was a courageous United States congressman who stood up for the rights of poor settlers and Native Americans alike. This was during the 1820s and 1830s—a period when most Americans were interested in claiming more western territories, not in being good neighbors to the people who had lived there for centuries.

But did Davy really kill a bear when he was just three years old? Did he "grin down" savage animals, armed only with his strong grip and irresistible charm? Did he never fail to hit the bulls-eye with "Ol' Betsy," his long rifle? Battle swamp 'gators? Teach a pet bear named "Death Hug" to smoke a pipe? Catch and wrestle a panther that had stolen his belongings?

Not likely. He became forever famous for such feats, though. And there may even have been a grain of truth at the heart of some of the fantastic stories that have been told about him.

Davy's ancestors were Irish immigrants who arrived in North Carolina before the American Revolution. His grandfather, David Crockett, moved into the frontier in the 1770s, settling in eastern Tennessee, where he and his wife were killed by warring Indians.

John and Rebecca Crockett, Davy's parents, built a farm on Big Limestone Creek in Greene County. Davy was born there on August 17, 1786. Large families were common in America's early years; Davy had eight brothers and sisters.

After failing as a hog farmer and miller, John Crockett opened a tavern on the wagon road between Knoxville, Tennessee, and Abingdon, Virginia. In those times, taverns functioned not only as places to buy food and drink but also as public meetinghouses and crude inns. Passing wagon drivers who craved a night's rest willingly slept three or four in a bed, with half a dozen or more to a room. As a boy, Davy began developing his storytelling skills while listening to the news and tall tales of travelers who ate and slept at the tavern.

He grew to be a skillful woodsman and hunter, and he was a strong, capable farm worker. In those

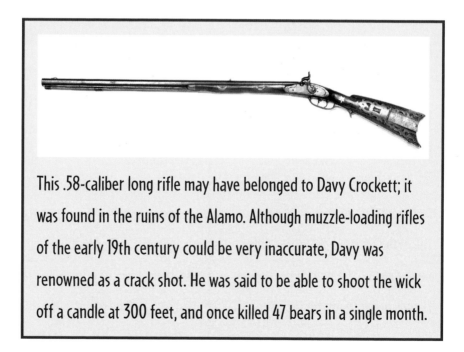

This .58-caliber long rifle may have belonged to Davy Crockett; it was found in the ruins of the Alamo. Although muzzle-loading rifles of the early 19th century could be very inaccurate, Davy was renowned as a crack shot. He was said to be able to shoot the wick off a candle at 300 feet, and once killed 47 bears in a single month.

days, Tennessee was a wild land. Relations with the Indians were uncertain; some Native Americans were quite friendly, but others were openly hostile. The forests were alive with panthers, bears, wolves, and other animals that raided farmyards and sometimes threatened the farmers themselves.

At 12, Davy helped a farmer drive a herd of cattle to Virginia. He earned $5 for his work—money badly needed by his struggling family. The farmer, though, tried to force him to remain in Virginia to work. At first, Davy agreed. But he was growing terribly homesick. Luckily, he soon met a neighbor from back home in Tennessee who agreed to smuggle him away in a wagon.

Davy arrived home safe, but he didn't remain there long. When Davy was 13, his father insisted he go to school. Davy soon

> In part, Davy learned his hunting skills through trial and error—and near tragedy. Once as a child, he fired his father's musket at what he thought was a deer moving through the brush. The musket ball found its mark—but to Davy's horror, it was no deer. It was a neighbor, picking berries in the forest. The man, shot through the lungs, lay feverishly near death for a long time, but to Davy's great relief, he survived.

made a powerful enemy: the school bully. The boy was older and larger, but Davy was much bolder. Davy vowed to "give him salt and vinegar"; he planned to punish the bully for pushing around the younger students.

He confronted the boy in the woods after school one day. "I scratched his face all to a flitter jig," Davy wrote later in his autobiography, "and soon made him cry out for quarters in good earnest."

When the schoolmaster learned of the fight, Davy knew, a whipping would be his own punishment. So he stayed away from school almost a week, spending each day roaming the woods. At last, however, the schoolmaster wrote a note to his father, inquiring where Davy was.

Davy's father was angrier than the schoolmaster and declared "he would whip me an eternal sight worse than the master," Davy recounted.

He figured his only option was to run away . . . but to where? The answer came to him almost immediately: he would head up the road to Virginia! This would take him far enough away to escape his father's wrath, but not so far that he couldn't return easily after the trouble had passed. He made his way to Virginia and found a job and a place to stay as a farmhand.

The lad was a hard worker and was thrifty with his meager earnings. He soon saved $7–a noteworthy sum 200 years ago. If he kept at his work, in a few years he might be able to buy his own farm or start a small business.

An unbridled spirit of adventure had already captivated the youth, though. At the moment, what he really wanted to do was see the ocean, perhaps even go to sea as a cabin boy. He went to Baltimore, one of the young nation's most important ports.

As things turned out, Davy never sailed the ocean. For about two years, he worked at various shore jobs. At last, in 1802, his yearning to see his family overcame his desire for independence–for the time being, at least. He made the long trip through Maryland and Virginia back to Crockett's Tavern.

He arrived late one evening. His family did not even recognize him because he'd grown so much. He said little, watching his relatives serve their *wagoner* guests and waiting to see if any of them would realize who he was. Finally, as everyone sat at the big table for supper, one of his sisters came around to him, overjoyed with amazement, and gave him a great hug.

Davy was angry at himself. "The joy of my sisters and my mother, and, indeed, of all the family, was such, that it humbled me, and made me sorry that I hadn't submitted to a hundred whippings, sooner than cause so much affliction as they had suffered on my account," he later wrote.

His father and mother were no longer angry at him. In fact, his father had gotten into serious debt and desperately needed Davy's help. The sturdy son dutifully went to work for nearby farmers until he earned enough to pay off John Crockett's heavy bills.

Schoolin' and Courtin'

As a young man, Davy Crockett lived in this cabin in Tennessee. As the frontier moved west over the years, Crockett would continue to move with it.

At age 18, Davy was a handsome, strong young man. His quick humor and gift for telling amusing stories made him very popular. Many a young woman had her eye on him—but they wondered if he would be willing to settle down. Soon, Davy was attracted to the young niece of his employer. He found to his dismay, however, that she had promised to marry someone else.

Perhaps, he reasoned, she had little respect for him because he was uneducated. Going back to school did not sound like fun, but Davy did just that, and it was a decision that would help him greatly later in life. For a nearly grown man who wanted to be outdoors, attending school was no easy task. But he kept at his studies for six months until he could read, write, and do simple arithmetic.

Schooling didn't result in quick success with the ladies, though. Another young woman broke up with him shortly before they were scheduled to be married. This second rejection was a great blow to his confidence. Maybe he was too rough and plain-spoken to suit well-mannered women, he thought. Maybe his funny but preposterous stories suggested

Unlike many of the men living on the frontier in the early 19th century, Davy Crockett had a basic education. This sample of his writing includes his favorite saying, "Be always sure you are right, then go ahead."

to them that he wasn't to be taken seriously. Or maybe they realized he probably wouldn't be content to stay in one place very long.

"My heart was bruised, and my spirits were broken down," Davy wrote of his second romantic breakup.

> So I bid her farewell, and turned my lonesome and miserable steps back again homeward, concluding that I was only born for hardships, misery, and disappointment. I now began to think that, in making me, it was entirely forgotten to make my mate, that I was born odd, and should always remain so, and nobody would have me. . . . I had no peace day nor night for several weeks. My appetite failed me, and I grew daily worse and worse. They all thought I was sick; and so I was. And it was the worst kind of sickness—a sickness of the heart, and all the tender parts, produced by disappointed love.

Then in 1806 he met Polly (Mary) Finley. He fell in love with her at a "reaping," an old-fashioned community dance party. Davy was pleased with her from the start. They danced and talked for a long time that night.

This time, the tables were turned in Davy's favor. Polly broke up with another young man in order to marry Davy. In a matter of weeks, their wedding was arranged.

The couple rented a farm and set out to build their life together on the frontier. Polly—"my little wife," as Davy referred to her—received several head of cattle from her parents as a wedding gift. Davy bought some simple furniture on

> After Davy and Polly were married, he admitted that he had been "afraid to wait long, for fear of another defeat."

credit from the general store. The next year, their first child was born; they named him John Wesley Crockett. Another son, William, and then a daughter, Margaret, came in 1809 and 1812.

By then, the family had moved west of the Appalachian Mountains, settling in southern Tennessee. The country was rich in game. Davy wrote: "It was here that I began to distinguish myself as a hunter." Plenty of deer, rabbits, and other small game were in the woods, and Davy put his long rifle—with which he reportedly could hit targets several hundred yards away—to good use. He found to his dismay, however, that the bears had been hunted almost to *extinction* in that area.

Soon, Davy's rifle would be aimed at human targets. Not far to the south, Creek Indians were on the brink of warfare against the white settlers.

Davy lived during the early days of America's westward expansion. Pioneer families were willing to settle in the wilderness, where they could work farmland of their own. As more and more of them moved west in **Conestoga wagons** and river **flatboats**, conflicts with the Native Americans seemed unavoidable. Many Americans believed the Indians should be forced to give up their territories. Although some Indians agreed to do this, others resisted, and tragedy resulted.

Settlers called the rebellious Creek Indians "Red Sticks," either because of their red-painted battle clubs or the red poles they put up in their villages.

In 1813, Creek warriors went on a rampage south of the Crocketts' Elk River country. The unrest occurred in what today is Alabama. White Americans on the frontier feared the Indians were being armed by Spanish and English enemies in the Southeast. White volunteers and Creek war parties began to set up ambushes and carry out surprise attacks against each other.

When a Red Stick war party overran Fort Mims in Alabama and massacred more than 500 settlers, the whites organized a **militia**. General Andrew Jackson was in command. The region was at war.

Like Davy Crockett, Andrew Jackson lived on the frontier in Tennessee. During the War of 1812, Jackson was the most successful American general, defeating the Creeks at Horseshoe Bend and driving the British from Pensacola, Florida.

FIGHTING RED STICKS AND REDCOATS

Davy signed up to be a militia scout. He proved his worth as a woodsman and tracker, although he had few occasions to distinguish himself as a fighting hero. What set him apart at the militia encampments was his story-telling. General Jackson himself remarked on Davy's ability to enliven camp life with his amusing tales.

When he did have to fight in battle, Davy found it

anything but amusing. In November, he was part of a force of 500 volunteers who crept up on a Creek village at a place called Tallusahatchee. Eager for revenge after the Fort Mims massacre, they attacked in a fury. More than 40 warriors were burned to death inside a hut. Men and women alike were slain. In all, some 200 Creek died that day—and memories of the bloodshed haunted Davy for many years.

Davy earned about $65 for serving three months with the army. That would be a small sum in today's workforce, but in 1813 it was an enormous amount. Polly was pleased with his earnings, but she was more pleased to have him home again just in time for Christmas.

She was not at all happy when he reenlisted the very next year. This time he would be gone six months, and he would be fighting a different enemy: the British.

Barely 30 years after winning its long war for independence, the United States was engaged in another struggle against the English redcoats. The War of 1812 was in its third year. In September 1814, Davy went to the far western region of Florida (sometimes called the Panhandle) as a sergeant with a unit called the Tennessee Mounted Gunmen.

Again, Davy earned no special honors as a soldier. He was involved in skirmishes with Seminole Indians, who sided with the British, but his greatest contribution to the American cause was his skill as a woodsman. He kept his unit supplied with wild game and honey during the autumn and winter.

The end of the war early in 1815 was a time for celebration. But for Davy, joy soon turned to grief. Polly came down with a deadly fever. Shortly after he arrived home, she died.

Davy was devastated. He was especially worried at the thought of his three children growing up without a mother's influence. So he invited his younger brother and sister-in-law to come live at the cabin with them. "They took as good care of my children as they well could," Davy recounted, "but yet it wasn't all like the care of a mother. And though their company was to me in every respect like that of a brother and sister, yet it fell far short of being like that of a wife. So I came to the conclusion it wouldn't do, but that I must have another wife."

By summer 1816, Davy had remarried. His second wife was Elizabeth Patton, widow of a farmer who had been killed in the recent Indian war and mother of two small children. "She was a good

The Battle of New Orleans, fought January 8, 1815, was one of the few American victories on land during the War of 1812. British casualties were more than 2,000 men; just 21 Americans were killed or wounded. The battle made Andrew Jackson a popular hero.

industrious woman, and owned a snug little farm, and lived quite comfortable," Davy said.

Elizabeth was a wise businesswoman as well as a loving wife and mother. Her "snug little farm" was no less than 200 acres. Elizabeth and her former husband had been quite prosperous, amassing a fortune of some $800 in cash. Davy had not only acquired a wonderful mate; he suddenly had become a prosperous farmer.

Yet, as in the past, he had more the mind of an explorer than of a farmer. Hardly had he and his children settled into their new home when Davy set out with several friends "to explore a new country." They crossed the Tennessee River and ventured southward, well into Creek territory.

The journey was filled with adventure and hardship. Soon after they left home, a poisonous snake bit one of Davy's companions. The group left the man at a frontier homestead to recuperate.

Then, while camped one night near present-day Tuscaloosa, Alabama, their horses ran off. As soon as it was daylight, Davy started in pursuit of them on foot, carrying his heavy rifle. All day, he waded through creeks and swamps and climbed mountains. Although he heard news of the horses at every house he passed, he couldn't catch up with them. At last, he realized he was never going to overtake them, and so he gave up the hunt. He turned back to the last house he had passed and stayed there till morning. "From the best calculation we could make," he wrote later, "I had walked over fifty miles that day; and the next morning I was so sore, and fatigued, that I felt like I couldn't walk any more."

Later, while walking back to rejoin his friends,

Davy became deathly sick. Some friendly Indians found him and helped him to a settler's cabin. There he lay helpless for weeks. Those attending him thought he would die any moment, but he gradually recovered. He found a ride with a wagoner and made his way home.

Repeated illness led Davy to believe that his family was living in an unhealthy region. So they packed their belongings in 1817 and moved into central Tennessee. Davy became a magistrate, a local judge. He later wrote, "If any one was charged with marking his neighbor's hogs, or with stealing anything—which happened pretty often in those days—I would have him taken [by a constable, or sheriff], and if there were tolerable grounds for the charge, I would have him well whipp'd and cleared."

Many of Davy and Elizabeth's relatives from eastern Tennessee moved out to this settlement,

> Davy wrote his autobiography in 1834. Considering his reputation as a sturdy, daring, unconquerable frontiersman, his descriptions of failures are surprising to read. While his book includes exaggerated portrayals of himself as a hero, it also reports his episodes of getting lost, falling sick, being afraid and rejected, and failing to accomplish things he set out to do.

called Shoal Creek. The log cabin community grew rapidly. The couple built a **gristmill** and did a brisk business grinding corn into meal for their neighbors. They also set up a whiskey *distillery* and a gunpowder factory.

Besides his duties as magistrate, Davy was appointed justice of the peace. This meant he now could perform marriages and handle taxes, as well as administer justice to common criminals. Then, the local militia elected him their colonel. This was undoubtedly his proudest achievement up to that point in his life.

But this was only the beginning. Davy was respected for his fair sentencing and was loved for his sense of humor. No one was surprised when the homespun woodsman's spiraling popularity soon led him into politics.

In his autobiography, Davy Crockett admitted that the idea of making political speeches made him weak-kneed and choked him up "as bad as if my mouth had been jamm'd and cramm'd chock full of dry mush."

BACKWOODS POLITICIAN

Davy had mixed feelings about running for public office. On the one hand, it was an exciting idea—a new kind of adventure. And he enjoyed being the center of attention. But on the other hand, the idea struck fear into the mind of the "fearless" pioneer. He knew nothing about government, politics, or making speeches. But, urged on by friends, he announced his candidacy

for the Tennessee State Legislature in early 1821–
then immediately left the state for a three-month
horse drive to North Carolina. When he returned,
he began looking for votes.

Davy's opponent considered the candidacy of
this "ignorant backwoods bear hunter" a joke. Davy
couldn't debate political issues. All he could do was tell his folksy stories at stump rallies and then invite the audience–mostly hard-scrabble farmers–to free drinks at the liquor stand. His rival usually

> The election process, and politics in general, were entirely new experiences for Davy. "A public document I had never seen," he confessed in his autobiography, "nor did I know there were such things; and how to begin I couldn't tell."

let Davy speak first, confident the frontiersman's
ignorance would be obvious to the people.

Surprisingly, that approach worked in Davy's
favor. At the rallies, by the time his opponent's turn
to speak came, the audience had dissolved, following Davy to the bar. His opponent had no one left to
listen to him, while the crowd was spellbound by
Davy's funny stories. Davy won the election by a
landslide and was off to Murfreesboro, then the state
capital.

His triumph quickly turned to despair. Almost as soon as he arrived in Murfreesboro, he received word that a flood had destroyed his gristmill. This did more than end his grinding business. Without his mill apparatus, he could not produce whiskey at his distillery. He recorded that "the misfortune just made a complete mash of me."

His wife, Elizabeth, led the family through the crisis, however. Many victims of such a disaster, Davy wrote, would have resorted to dishonest means to get back on their feet. But Elizabeth insisted that Davy pay the people to whom he owed money. "Just pay up, as long as you have a bit's worth in the world," she advised her husband. "And then everybody will be satisfied, and we will scuffle for more."

The Crocketts sold what they had left, moved farther into the frontier, and started a new farm. Davy helped support his family by hunting for food and selling wild animal furs. He was already an excellent shot, and he improved his skills with the help of "Ol' Betsy," a long rifle some friends gave him in 1822.

But the return to his pioneering ways didn't remove him from politics for long. This time, he

After losing his gristmill in a flood shortly after being elected to the Tennessee legislature, Davy Crockett and his wife, Elizabeth, sold their farm and moved to a new homestead farther out on the Tennessee frontier.

wasn't merely *encouraged* to run for the legislature; he practically was *forced* to run.

While Davy was socializing with some old soldiers and country politicians in Jackson, Tennessee, someone suggested that he should run for another term in the legislature. He replied that he now "lived at least forty miles from any white settlement" and "had no thought of becoming a candidate." But a week later, a local newspaper reported that Davy would run for office again.

Apparently, the newspaper article was a practical joke played on him by some of his friends. However, it served to renew Davy's desire for "electioneering." This time, he campaigned against an influential doctor in the area. Again, his down-to-earth popularity got him elected.

One thing that made Davy so well liked was that he knew little more about the workings of government than the uneducated farmers and traders who elected him. His ignorance actually worked to his advantage. The voters felt he truly was one of them.

In his book, he described one of the first conversations he had with some of his fellow legislators. They were discussing the appointments of judges—the judiciary branch of government. Davy hastily excused himself and left. "I was afraid some one would ask me what the judiciary was; and if I knowed I wish I may be shot. I don't indeed believe I had ever before heard that there was any such thing in all nature."

Another story from his autobiography recalled a campaign stop in an unfamiliar neck of the woods.

"Here they told me that they wanted to move their town nearer to the center of the county, and I must come out in favor of it," Davy wrote. "There's no devil if I knowed what this meant, or how the town was to be moved; and so I kept dark."

But despite his inexperience, from the beginning of his statesman's career Davy stood for the rights of hard-working common folk. One tense issue in Tennessee was property ownership. Laws guarantee rightful ownership today, but in Davy's time land ownership could be questionable. Revolutionary War veterans in North Carolina, for example, were allowed to claim certain lands in Tennessee. Some of this property had been developed into thriving farms by toiling pioneer families. Davy fought for years to preserve the settlers' claims, but ultimately he was unsuccessful.

He also opposed what he considered excessive government taxation and interference in the every-day affairs of citizens. For instance, he voted against a bill that would outlaw gambling. He believed such matters were a person's private business.

Andrew Jackson, Davy's old army commander, had become a leading politician in Tennessee and was a contender for national office. Davy felt an

This 19th-century woodcut shows Davy Crockett giving a campaign speech to a cheering crowd in front of a backwoods saloon.

attachment to the general, but the two men did not always see eye to eye on political matters. Davy was one of the few Tennessee statesmen who did not hesitate to oppose Jackson when it came to a vote. This attitude in time would doom Davy's political career, but it added to his reputation for honesty. "I let the people know . . . that I wouldn't take a collar around my neck," he wrote later.

After four years in the state assembly, Davy was recognized as a strong prospect for national office. "The gentleman from the cane," as he was called in

When Davy Crockett was urged by some of the people of Tennessee to run for the U.S. Congress in the 1825 election, he at first declined. He did not feel that he was smart enough, he wrote in his autobiography. "At last I was called on by a good many to be a candidate," he said. "I told the people that I couldn't stand that; it was a step above my knowledge, and I know'd nothing about Congress matters. However, I was obliged to agree to run."

the legislature, was the leader people turned to when they became dissatisfied with their congressman, Adam Alexander, in 1825.

In many elections, *economic* issues are the deciding factors for voters. So it was in western Tennessee in 1825. The price of cotton soared. This meant that the farmers in the territory. would make more money from their crops. Congressman Alexander took credit for the favorable cotton prices. During the campaign Alexander persuaded the majority of Tennessee voters that he was the candidate who would ensure continued prosperity. Davy lost the election.

Davy was disappointed, but he made plans to oppose Alexander in the next election, which was two years away. In his autobiography, Davy noted that Alexander "went on, and served out his term, and at the end of it cotton was down . . . again; and I concluded I would try him once more, and see how it would go with cotton at the common price."

But first, Davy wanted a recess from politics. While waiting for the next election, he devoted the next two years to his first loves: hunting and trying new wilderness ventures.

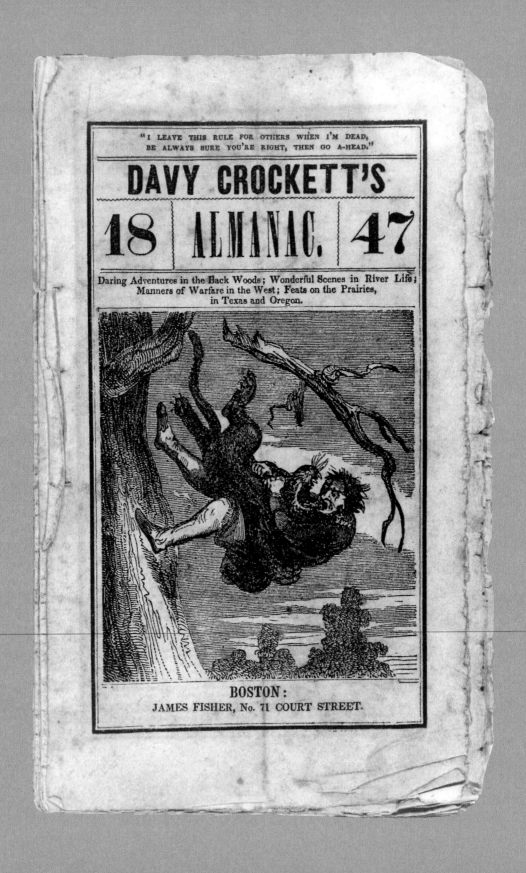

"I LEAVE THIS RULE FOR OTHERS WHEN I'M DEAD,
BE ALWAYS SURE YOU'RE RIGHT, THEN GO A-HEAD."

DAVY CROCKETT'S

18 ALMANAC. 47

Daring Adventures in the Back Woods; Wonderful Scenes in River Life;
Manners of Warfare in the West; Feats on the Prairies,
in Texas and Oregon.

BOSTON:
JAMES FISHER, No. 71 COURT STREET.

By the end of Crockett's time in Congress, his exploits had become legendary. Beginning in 1836, a number of publishers brought out almanacs bearing his name. In addition to weather information and farming tips, these almanacs included fanciful stories about Crockett's adventures. This cover from an 1847 almanac shows him wrestling with a wildcat in a tree.

FROM CALAMITY TO CONGRESS

The most exciting tales told about Davy Crockett are those of his bear hunts in the Tennessee wilderness. Surprisingly, historians believe they're true—for the most part, at least.

Between his congressional campaigns, Davy set a crew to building cargo boats on a lake. They also cut and trimmed wood strips for use in making kegs. The plan was to transport a large shipment of these wooden **staves** down the Mississippi River to New Orleans, where Davy expected to earn a handsome profit. The project would take months. But despite his log-cutting and carpentry he still made time to hunt game. And his favorite prey was bear.

He reported killing 15 of the fierce (but awkwardly fat) animals in a two-week period—on the average, a bear a day. One day, he wrote, he and his young son, with a pack of fine hunting dogs, took three bears in half an hour.

The episode began when their dogs picked up a scent and went charging out of sight through a canebrake. As Davy stood listening, he realized his dogs had split into two groups, and both were fighting. He sent his young son after one group of dogs, while he ran after the other. He found the dogs had a two-year-old bear down on the ground; without even firing his gun, Davy snatched out his butcher knife and thrust it into the bear. A few moments later, he heard a gunshot; his son had also killed a bear.

While they were exchanging stories, they heard a dog begin to bark, and the other dogs took off. Davy and his son followed and found the biggest bear of all up in a tree. They shot and killed that bear as well.

Soon afterward, in the dead of winter, Davy almost froze to death. Hunting alone with his dogs, he found himself tangling with a ferocious bear late into the night. By the time the fight was over and the bear was slain, Davy's clothes were wet and the temperature was below freezing. Dry wood was scarce, and his campfire was a feeble one. Davy knew he would freeze to death if he didn't warm himself up, so he jumped up and down and shouted and threw himself around.

Despite all his efforts, he was still shaking with cold, and now he was so tired he could barely walk. At last, he got an idea. He found a tree with a two-foot thick trunk and no limbs for 30 feet; over and over, he shimmied up the tree and then slid down to the bottom again. The friction warmed his legs and arms, keeping him from freezing. By the time the sun rose, Davy had lost count of how many times he had climbed that tree and slid down again. He was sure, though, that he must have done it at least 100 times.

Before long, though, another adventure had him in far worse danger. With his boats completed and his supply of staves bundled aboard, he and his men took to the river. Disaster waited for them on the

Mississippi at a bend called the Devil's Elbow. "If any place in the wide creation has its own proper name," Davy recalled, "I thought it was this. Here we had about the hardest work that I ever was engaged in, in my entire life, to keep out of danger."

They tried to steer the boats out of the treacherous waters toward shore, but the current was too powerful. Sometime in the night, Davy was down in the cabin of one of the boats, sitting by the fire, thinking about what a mess they had gotten into. Just as he was thinking about how much better it was to be bear-hunting on solid land than to be facing the water's dangers, the hatchway into the cabin slapped down, right through the top of the boat. The boat was now floating sideways. Then Davy heard the men begin to run over the top of the boat. They pulled with all their might, but the boat slammed broadside against the head of an island. Davy jumped up and tried to escape from the sinking boat, but the water was pouring through the hole in the boat's side in a current so strong that Davy could not push against it.

He tried to squirm through a small paddle hole in the side of the boat cabin—and got stuck! He did the only thing he could: he bellowed for help as loudly as he could. Some of his crew heard him and grabbed him by the arms. With a violent effort, they jerked him through the hole. Later, he recalled, "I was literally skin'd like a rabbit."

He lost his entire shipment of barrel staves to the unforgiving Mississippi. But he still had his life, his backwoods spunk, and his ever-growing reputation. And Congressman Alexander was coming up for reelection.

It was a four-candidate race this time—and a bruiser of a political battle. One of his opponents accused Davy of drunkenness. Davy fought back with vicious accusations of his own. Otherwise, though, Davy's opponents ignored him. He may have charmed his way into the state legislature, they figured, but he amounted to little as a candidate for national office.

Davy surprised them—and some of his own supporters—by winning the 1827 election. He went to Congress in Washington, D.C., dressed in "city clothes," but as an avowed backcountry supporter of Andrew Jackson, who had become the working folks' candidate for president. He openly opposed Jackson, however, in certain matters.

His first term in Congress was not without

mistakes. Davy often was bored with the long, sometimes confusing, and almost pointless speeches of his colleagues. When he began to yawn, he reportedly would wander out of the hallowed congressional chamber to have a drink at a nearby pub. He missed dozens of congressional votes in which he should have promoted his state's views.

When basic issues were being debated, though, Davy steadfastly stood for the ragged, rugged farmers of the frontier. He fought to ensure the rights of farm owners against the money-making schemes of speculators, wily businessmen who plotted to get rich on shady land deals in the frontier territories.

Interestingly, this put him at serious odds with Andrew Jackson. Jackson began to suspect Davy was more an opponent than a supporter. Davy Crockett the congressman was not playing politics the Washington way. Jackson even worried that Davy might become more popular in his home state than Jackson was himself.

Davy was easily reelected and resumed his congressional seat in 1829. But powerful political forces were working against him. Jackson had won the presidency that year; he was a personal friend of Davy's, but Jackson's political allies believed that

This watercolor painting of Davy Crockett was made when he was serving as a congressman in Washington, D.C.

Davy was as much of a threat in Congress as a loose cannon would be on the rolling deck of a ship at sea.

Davy eventually became an outspoken opponent of the Jackson *agenda* in Washington. At the same time, he made few allies in other quarters. Davy wanted the government to award retirement pay to Revolutionary War militia volunteers, as well as to Continental Army regulars; Congress refused. He criticized West Point, which he considered a military academy where only wealthy youth were appointed, youth who knew nothing of frontier fighting. He argued that West Point should be abandoned, but few government officials paid him serious attention.

His most outrageous opposition, in the minds of Jackson supporters, was his fight against a scheme to

Herded by U.S. troops, Cherokee Indians are forced to move from their homes in Georgia to the Indian Territory (Oklahoma) during the 1830s. The long route west became known as the Trail of Tears. Although Davy Crockett had come to Washington as a supporter of President Andrew Jackson, he disagreed with the Indian policy and soon found himself opposed to the Jackson administration.

relocate several Native American tribes. Jackson's forces wanted to drive the Indians westward, far from the bulging frontier. This would open more land for poor European-American farmers—Davy's *grassroots* friends. But this action would be unfair to the Indians, Davy decided. He called the natives a "once powerful people" whose "only chance of aid was at the hands of Congress. Should its members turn a deaf ear to their cries, misery must be their fate."

When he came up for reelection in 1831, Davy was portrayed as a drunken gambler who frequently missed legislative sessions. Davy's attendance record in Congress was dismal, but his opponent's charges of drunkenness and wild living probably went too far. Still, enough voters lost faith in Davy that they gave the congressional seat to a lawyer, William Fitzgerald.

Two years later, Davy again ran for Congress. This time, a poor cotton economy was in his favor. He was sent to Washington for a third term.

During this session, he was mentioned as a possible future candidate for president of the United States. His reputation for honesty and independence had impressed the Whig Party. Most historians doubt the Whigs seriously intended to promote Davy for president; they merely wanted to borrow his popularity in their political battles against Andrew Jackson. Davy probably understood this— and perhaps used the Whigs' high-minded talk about him to help promote his new project.

By this time, the name of Davy Crockett excited

As Crockett became more openly opposed to the leadership of Jackson and his vice president, Martin Van Buren, the two men made it harder for Davy to accomplish anything in Congress. Some people thought Crockett might challenge Van Buren for the presidency in the 1836 election.

Americans throughout the East. Davy took advantage of his popularity; with the help of a friend, he had written his autobiography. It became a bestseller (this was quite remarkable, since its author was a man of poor grammar who had attended school less than one year).

Meanwhile, a play titled *The Lion of the West* had begun making the rounds of big-city theaters. The play depicted a character named "Nimrod Wildfire," and the production was clearly based on Davy and his exploits. Davy was not comfortable going to the theater, but he turned out to see this play in Washington—and exchanged public bows with the actor who portrayed him.

He went on a speaking tour throughout the Northeast and was greeted enthusiastically at every stop. People were eager to listen to the frontier politician whose astonishing deeds—whether true or exaggerated—were being publicized far and wide.

His national popularity made him a hero for all time, but it did not ensure his political future. In 1835, his career as a statesman reached its climax. Davy Crockett, now almost 50 years old, was at the crossroads of his life.

Texas

6

Crockett is depicted here at the center of the Texas soldiers, defending the Alamo's southeast wall in the final rush of Santa Anna's overwhelming military force. The 1,800-man Mexican army outnumbered the Texans 10 to 1 when they attacked at dawn on March 6, 1836.

When his congressional seat came up for reelection in 1835, Davy campaigned hard to keep it. But his heart was no longer in Washington—if, really, it ever had been. As always, he had one eye on the western frontier. And by this time, his attention was drawn very far to the west: Texas.

Davy had become discouraged by the federal government. He was especially unhappy with President Jackson, who he believed was more interested in holding onto power than in helping common Americans. The people who kept the president and his political friends in power, Davy was convinced, were dishonest and selfish.

Challenging Davy for Congress in 1835 was another "Jackson man," Adam Huntsman. Huntsman, a respected veteran of the War of 1812, was slowed physically by a wooden leg, but he was an aggressive campaigner. He repeated the charges of Davy's long-time enemies, claiming that Davy was given to excessive drinking and otherwise care-less behavior. Huntsman received heavy support from the Jackson *faction* in Washington.

Huntsman won the election. Davy believed his foes literally "bought" the vote, paying citizens in cash to turn against him. "For fourteen years since I have been a candidate," Davy wrote afterward, "I never saw such means used to defeat any candidate, as were put in practice against me on this occasion."

In just two years, his defeat would be avenged when his son John Wesley Crockett won a seat in Congress. But Davy was terribly bitter at the politi-cal system. The key to getting elected, he joked, was to "promise all that is asked, and more if you can think of anything."

After his loss, Davy declared that he was "done with politics for the present." He almost immediately set out for Texas, accompanied by several relatives and other frontiersmen. Perhaps in Texas–a region outside U.S. boundaries, occupied by pioneers with independent spirits–he would find a new beginning, not just for himself but for others who desired plain self-government.

Davy and his friends traveled southwest by horseback and steamboat. When they arrived in eastern Texas, instantly he liked what he saw in the Red River Valley. Perhaps, he thought, this would

When Davy Crockett arrived in Texas, the area was part of Mexico. At the time, Mexico was ruled by General Antonio López de Santa Anna, who had established a dictatorship. Santa Anna was a skilled military strategist.

William Travis, commander of the Alamo defenders, believed his small force would be reinforced before the Mexican army reached the fort. However, Santa Anna's troops arrived in late February and began blasting the walls with cannons. In a dispatch sent on February 24, 1836, the first day of the siege, Travis promised to fight until "victory or death."

be a good place to make a new home. In time, members of his family also relocated to Texas.

This was an extremely tense moment in Texas history, however. Texas was controlled by Mexico, but American-born residents there—the majority of Texans—were clamoring for independence. With his reputation for bravery and his homespun popularity, Davy was expected to join the cause for a free Texas. The people of Texas greeted him with excitement. If fighting broke out, they believed, he would be a natural leader. He and his companions swore pledges of loyalty to Texas.

Davy was eager to join the freedom fighters

when Santa Anna, the Mexican president, marched on San Antonio with an army of several thousand in February 1836. Led by Colonel William Barrett Travis, 183 Texans waited at the Alamo, an old Spanish mission near San Antonio that had hastily been turned into a fortress. Davy Crockett was among them.

He wasn't the only frontier hero at the Alamo. Already waiting with the other freedom fighters when he arrived was Jim Bowie, an adventurer who had become an American legend in his own right. Bowie had perfected a type of hunting knife that was named after him. It seemed fitting that two of

Jim Bowie was a 40-year-old adventurer, whose claim to fame was the creation of a large hunting knife popularly called the bowie knife. Bowie seemed to welcome a last stand at the Alamo. "We will rather die in these ditches than give it up to the enemy," he wrote.

America's most famous backwoodsmen would join company in the epic battle.

Sam Houston, commander of all the Texan forces, ordered Travis to abandon the Alamo. Houston knew the complex could not be defended for long against such a large Mexican army. But Travis refused to move. "Victory or death!" he vowed defiantly.

The blue and white uniforms of the Mexican Army came into view on February 23, 1836. If the Texans did not surrender, Santa Anna warned, they would be given "no quarter" but would be killed to the last man. The Texans stood firm.

Santa Anna ordered a bombardment, then massive attacks. One wave of Mexicans was beaten back with heavy losses, then another.

> After the battle, a Mexican captain named Rafael Soldana described a defender who may have been Davy Crockett. "He wore a buckskin suit and a cap," wrote Soldana. "This man would rest his long gun and fire, and we all learned to keep at a good distance when he was seen to make ready to shoot. He rarely missed his mark, and when he fired he always rose to his feet and calmly reloaded his gun, seemingly indifferent to the shots fired at him by our men. . . . This man I later learned was known as 'Kwockey.'"

But the defenders were being slain and wounded, too, and they were running out of ammunition. For almost two weeks they held out grimly, hoping for reinforcements. But help never came.

In a final assault, blue-coated soldiers with scaling ladders began to fight their way over the walls between the thinning ranks of Texans. On March 6, the last defender was killed and the Mexicans held the Alamo.

Historians believe the hero from Tennessee was one of the last defenders to die. According to legend, his body was found among some 20 enemy corpses; his gun, Ol' Betsy, was bloodied and broken from the final moments of hand-to-hand fighting.

Mexican witnesses provide another account. When Davy and the few remaining Texans ran out of rifle balls and powder, they reportedly put down their guns and surrendered. A Mexican general promised them fair treatment as prisoners of war. But Santa Anna had other plans. He quickly ordered the captives executed. Mexican officers reportedly slew them with swords, then burned the mangled bodies.

The Mexicans' triumph was short-lived. When word spread of the slaughter at the Alamo, Texans

After the slaughter of the fort's defenders, "Remember the Alamo" became a rallying cry for independence. Six weeks later, the Texans destroyed Santa Anna's army at the Battle of San Jacinto.

were more determined than ever to win their independence. The following month, a ragtag force led by Houston annihilated the main Mexican army at the Battle of San Jacinto and captured Santa Anna. "Remember the Alamo!" was their victory cry. Soon afterward, Texas became a nation (and later, of course, a state of the Union).

Today, "Remember the Alamo!" still reminds Americans of the historic battle near San Antonio. To many, it summons the image of Davy Crockett, whose spectacular life and brutal death have been the subject of movies, television serials, plays, and songs. But serious students of frontier history remember Davy by a different slogan—the one he lived by. Whenever you're facing a tough decision, he advised, "be always sure you're right—then go ahead!"

Throughout his life, he applied the motto in all types of situations: courting, hunting, exploring, "electioneering," and joining the Texans in their bloody fight against Santa Anna. He had many faults—bragging, leaving his wife and family for long periods to explore new lands, improving his personal image on tour while neglecting congressional business, perhaps enjoying himself a bit too much over whiskey with his friends. But he always stood fast for the important issues he believed were right.

The story of Davy Crockett is one of ups and downs, triumphs and tragedies. He endured severe illnesses and family tragedies, lost his possessions more than once, left politics in final defeat, and lost his life in battle. To the end, though, he kept his sense of humor and his belief that he could bounce back from any calamity—by honest means. He lives in history as possibly America's best-loved and most-respected pioneer.

CHRONOLOGY

1786 Davy Crockett is born in eastern Tennessee on August 17

1798 At 12, travels to Virginia, helping drive a herd of cattle

1799 Threatened with punishment after a school fight, runs away from home

1806 Marries Polly Finley

1813 With Creek Indians on the warpath, becomes a scout in the settlers' volunteer army

1814 Serves as a scout under General Andrew Jackson
-15 during the War of 1812

1816 After the death of Polly, marries Elizabeth Patton

1821 Elected to the Tennessee State Legislature

1822 Loses his mill in a flood and moves to a new farm on the frontier

1823 Elected to the Tennessee State Legislature

1825 Makes unsuccessful bid for seat in US Congress

1826 Nearly drowns when his cargo boats wreck on a journey down the Mississippi

1827 Elected to the U.S. Congress, the first of three two-year terms he will serve

1834 After being elected to a third term in Congress, writes his autobiography and goes on a speaking tour

1835 Defeated in his reelection bid, decides to leave his career and family and relocate in Texas territory

1836 Killed at the Alamo on March 6

agenda—a planned political program; a list of things to be accomplished.

buckskin—animal hides, often used to make clothes.

Conestoga wagon—a horse- or mule-drawn covered wagon used by pioneers to carry their belongings westward.

distillery—a factory where liquor is extracted from solid produce.

economic—having to do with money matters.

extinction—the elimination of (usually) a species of wildlife, altogether or from a certain habitat it once occupied.

faction—a party or group within the government.

flatboats—flat-bottomed, usually rectangular work boats used to transport freight along rivers and other shallow waters.

grassroots—having to do with the basic, most fundamental level of society, the common people.

gristmill—a mill, usually powered by water-driven wheels, where corn and other grains are ground into meal, flour, and other food products.

militia—a local or regional military force called to duty only in times of emergency, as distinguished from the army of full-time "regular" soldiers.

staves—narrow strips of wood used to construct the sides of containers such as barrels.

wagoner—a person who transported products in frontier times, using a crude, sturdy, horse- or mule-drawn wagon.

Further Reading

Blair, Walter. *Davy Crockett: Legendary Frontier Hero*. Springfield, Ill.: Lincoln-Herndon, 1986.

Burke, James Wakefield. *David Crockett: The Man Behind the Myth*. Austin, Tex.: Eakin, 1984.

Crockett, David. *The Life of David Crockett, The Original Humorist and Irrepressible Backwoodsman: An Autobiography* [reprint]. New York: A.L. Burt Company, 1902.

Derr, Mark. *The Frontiersman: The Real Life and the Many Legends of Davy Crockett*. New York: William Morrow and Company, 1993.

Lofaro, Michael A., ed. *Davy Crockett: The Man, the Legend, the Legacy, 1786-1986*. Knoxville: University of Tennessee Press, 1985.

Moseley, Elizabeth R. *Davy Crockett: Hero of the Wild Frontier*. New York: Chelsea, 1991.

Sanford, William R., and Carl R. Green. *Davy Crockett: Defender of the Alamo*. Springfield, N.J.: Enslow, 1996.

Shackford, James Atkins. *David Crockett: The Man and the Legend*. Chapel Hill: University of North Carolina Press, 1986.

PICTURE CREDITS

DANIEL E. HARMON is associate editor of *Sandlapper: The Magazine of South Carolina* and editor of *The Lawyer's PC,* a national computer newsletter. He is the author of 26 books, most of them nonfiction historical and humorous works and biographies. Harmon lives in Spartanburg, South Carolina.